AMERICAN ARTISTS

ANSEL ADAMS:
THE SPIRIT OF WILD PLACES

EDWARD HOPPER:
A MODERN MASTER

FRANK LLOYD WRIGHT:
FORCE OF NATURE

GEORGIA O'KEEFE:
AN ETERNAL SPIRIT

GRANDMA MOSES:
AN AMERICAN ORIGINAL

MARY CASSATT:
AN AMERICAN IMPRESSIONIST

THE HUDSON RIVER SCHOOL:
AMERICAN LANDSCAPE ARTISTS

THE LEGACY OF NORMAN ROCKWELL

THE
HUDSON RIVER
SCHOOL

AMERICAN LANDSCAPE ARTISTS

BERT D. YAEGER

ABOUT THE AUTHOR

BERT D. YAEGER is a graduate of Antioch College where he recieved a degree in philosophy. As an editor and writer, he has specialized not only in the fine arts but in social sciences and the history of ideas and has contributed to a work on the French Revolution. He currently lives in New York City where he is an editor at St. Martin's Press.

MASON CREST

MASON CREST
450 Parkway Drive, Suite D
Broomall, Pennsylvania 19008
(866) MCP-BOOK (toll-free)

First printing
9 8 7 6 5 4 3 2 1

ISBN (hardback) 978-1-4222-4157-8
ISBN (series) 978-1-4222-4154-7
ISBN (ebook) 978-1-4222-7645-7

Cataloging-in-Publication Data on file with the Library of Congress

QR CODES AND LINKS TO THIRD-PARTY CONTENT
You may gain access to certain third-party content ("Third-Party Sites") by scanning and using the QR Codes that appear in this publication (the "QR Codes"). We do not operate or control in any respect any information, products, or services on such Third-Party Sites linked to by us via the QR Codes included in this publication, and we assume no responsibility for any materials you may access using the QR Codes. Your use of the QR Codes may be subject to terms, limitations or restrictions set forth in the applicable terms of use or otherwise established by the owners of the Third-Party Sites. Our linking to such Third-Party Sites via the QR Codes does not imply an endorsement or sponsorship of such Third-Party Sites, or the information, products, or services offered on or through the Third- Party Sites, nor does it imply an endorsement or sponsorship of this publication by the owners of such Third-Party Sites.

PHOTO CREDITS

CONTENTS

INTRODUCTION

THE GREAT OBJECT

Our scenery is the great object which attracts foreign tourists to our shores.
No blind adherence to authority here checks the hand or chills the heart of the artist.
HENRY T. TUCKERMAN, 1867

In 1819, a young Englishman named Thomas Cole emigrated to the United States only five years after the Treaty of Ghent concluded the War of 1812 between Americans and his former countrymen. Sixteen years later, he had established himself as the premier painter of the American wilderness, and his work would affect the American way of seeing for half a century. Cole was not unaware of the disruptive effects of the Industrial Revolution in England, the devastating, politically inspired violence released by the toppling of the *ancien régime* in France, and the ensuing rampages of Napoleon I's armies. If not actually conservative, he was certainly cautious in the spirit of the conservationist observing the decline of an ecosystem. The nineteenth-century painter, who today is generally recognized as holding the iconic status of having founded what came to be called the Hudson River School, acknowledged urban life and industry as encroaching inevitabilities.

Cole's beloved natural kingdom continues to recede from view, and, as he appeared to understand so acutely, it has come to occupy less and less space in the images made by successive generations. He was perhaps prematurely nostalgic when he pondered that, as art eventually was taken out of nature, nature would be taken out of art.

Cole's painting had been a kind of prospecting after the sublime, and the America he found in the region of the Hudson River valley amply rewarded that pursuit. His technique, however, would require an aesthetic intelligence that could not permit anything like complete insulation from the European masters.

The Course of Empire: The Savage State

THOMAS COLE. *1833; detail. New York Historical Society.*

With windblown mist and smoke from the aboriginal encampment, Cole has enhanced an impression of menace in this landscape. A curling mass of clouds unfurls to reveal primitive humans scurrying in the emerald wilderness. A tree in the lower left mimics the mountain peak emerging from the fog.

The Clove, Catskills
THOMAS COLE. *c. 1827; oil on canvas;*
25 x 33 in. (64 x 84 cm). New Britain
Museum of American Art, Connecticut.
Charles F. Smith Fund.
In this example of his early studies of
the Catskills, Cole has used a favorite
composition in which downward angles
of tree-covered mountains form the
v-shape of the ravine. The slope in the
foreground is in shadow, while sunlight
falls on the ravine. Rock formations
and a crooked tree introduce the
view, while gray clouds sweep the sky.

Even if James Fenimore Cooper, in his 1823 novel *The Pioneers*, gave his frontier hero Natty Bumppo the capability to exult in America's scenery—an enthusiasm that surpassed mere love of the great outdoors—there were technical and intellectual influences that were not to be found among rough-and-ready frontier explorers and settlers. Like many American artists after him, Cole would have to borrow vitally important tradition from an older world in order to translate into substantive works of art the natural world that a new and impatient civilization was settling.

Cole noted the paradox of the American artist's unique position of being able to catalogue an unfolding panorama of awe-inspiring natural phenomena in a virginal land while having little history or lore with which to establish a symbolic foundation. In his often brooding "Essay on American Scenery" (1835), he faced the American landscape's lack of an aesthetic past and apparently limited thematic resources, tersely arguing: "But American

associations are not so much of the past as of the present and future."

It was, arguably, America's fledgling literary community that first gave encouragement and, on occasion, considerable inspiration to the visual artists of Cole's generation. James Fenimore Cooper and Washington Irving were two of the most prominent representatives of this initial wave of enthusiasts. As literary artists, Cooper and Irving, in their examination of the country's towns, frontier outposts, and still untamed or newly discovered territory, were intent upon expanding the horizons of an American cultural self-awareness.

Italian Landscape

WASHINGTON ALLSTON. *c. 1805; oil on canvas; 40 x 50 3/4 in. (102 x 129 cm).*
Addison Gallery of Art, Phillips Academy, Andover, Massachusetts.
While in Rome, Allston noted that the sixteenth-century Venetian masters Titian, Tintoretto, and Veronese "leave the subject to be made by the spectator, provided he possessed the imaginative faculty." An example of Allston's mastery of neo-classicism, this landscape also shows signs of his distinctive rendering of clouds.

Following page:
Diana in the Chase

WASHINGTON ALLSTON. *1805; oil on canvas; 65 5/8 x 97 5/8 in. (167 x 248 cm).*
President and Fellows, Harvard College, Harvard University Art Museums. Gift of Mrs. Edward W. Moore. Allston painted this large landscape while in Rome. It constituted a breakthrough for Allston toward Romanticism and for American art by elevating the role of mood in landscape. Rather than portray mere topographical detail, Allston builds an edifice of composition with stark mountains and an intensely expressive sky.

Landscape Scene from the Last of the Mohicans

THOMAS COLE. *1827; oil on canvas; 25 x 31 in. (64 x 79 cm). New York State Historical Association, Cooperstown.* Cole pictorially interpreted few specific literary sources, but James Fenimore Cooper's *The Last of the Mohicans* was set in the Hudson River Valley and Lake George region—Cole's metier. The tense action takes place on a mountain ledge, with immense boulders, trees aflame with autumn, and barren crags forming a rugged amphitheater.

Expulsion from the Garden of Eden

THOMAS COLE. *c. 1827-1828; detail. Gift of Mrs. Maxim Karolik for the M. and M. Karolik Collection of American Paintings, 1815-1865. Museum of Fine Arts, Boston.* Cole employed the topographical vocabulary of landscape for visualizing banishment from divinely created paradise. As in *The Voyage of Life*, a cavern-like gate signifies transition. An abject Adam and Eve venture into the barren world "east of Eden," where Cole has placed an erupting volcano in a circle of clouds.

While the majority of those painters who have come to be regarded as integral members of the Hudson River School dutifully traveled to Europe to study—or had been trained there before immigrating to America—a definite sense of what it was to be an American artist was imperative. An unequivocal identity that could be found in American painters' subjects as well as their methods began to gain a foothold when the fantasist Washington Irving, in a country too young to have evolved much of a folklore, set out to create one, thus reversing the usual process of turning traditional tales into literature.

**The Return of
Rip Van Winkle**
JOHN QUIDOR. *1829;
oil on canvas; 39 1/4 x 49 3/4.
(100 x 126 cm). National
Gallery of Art, Washington.
Andrew Mellon Collection, 1942.*
Quidor found the perfect
foil for his unique style in
Washington Irving's *The Sketch
Book*. Influenced by eighteenth-
century English caricaturist
John Rowlandson, Quidor
developed an eerie and
macabre world in which
eyes protrude and faces
are twisted on the verge of
lunacy. Here, Rip Van Winkle
claims not to know who he is.

A New Pantheon

In 1809 Irving unveiled his recognition of the problem in his *Knickerbocker's History of New York:* "How convenient it would be to . . . our great men and great families of doubtful origin, could they have the privilege of the heroes of yore, who, whenever their origin was involved in obscurity, modestly announced themselves descended from a god."

As the pseudonymous Diedrich Knicker-bocker, Irving took American self-consciousness and recognition of uniquely American regional types and produced a mythology for a new world in answer to the old world's classical one. This mythopoeic effort to make up for America's sparse folklore formed the first steps in a process that would also establish a basis for a national sense of nature's sublimity, an occasionally rigid belief that would serve to embolden the Hudson River School's concentrated attention on American scenery and legitimize both the content and interpretations advanced by the school's numerous followers.

An American Romantic

In 1801, the year Cole was born in Bolton-le-Moor, Lancashire, England, the American painter Washington Allston was studying in London with his compatriot Benjamin West at the Royal Academy. The American-born West had been appointed president of the institution in 1792, a position he held until his death in 1820. It was Allston who introduced an unusual combination of Classicism and ominous Romanticism to an austere and censorious American audience.

Allston's education abroad, which continued until 1808, was not confined to London. In 1803 the artist went to Paris to take in the Louvre, and in 1804 he traveled to Rome, where the accomplishments of the Venetian masters proved to have a decided effect on his early figural compositions. The landscapes Allston produced while in Rome showed that he had consolidated his mastery of both approved styles and traditional scenic elements—the Italian Alps, the pines of Rome, and the campagna.

Following his return to England in 1811, his award-winning exhibition of the imposing *The Dead Man Restored to Life by Touching the Bones of the Prophet Elisha* at the British Institution failed to dissuade Allston from sailing back, in 1818, to America, where he settled in Boston.

With his massive *Belshazzar's Feast* left unfinished and highly experimental *Elijah in the Desert* (1817–1818) shunned by collectors for not toeing the moral line of Unitarian Boston, Allston had this to say after encountering the young Thomas Cole: "He has chosen a profession in itself innocent, and if properly pursued— that is, for its own sake—in a high degree elevating. Indeed it seems as if no one could truly love nature without loving its divine author, who in all His works, even in the horrible, no less than in the beautiful, speaks only in the language of love."

Elijah in the Desert

WASHINGTON ALLSTON. *1818; oil on canvas; 48 3/4 x 72 1/2 in. (124 x 184 cm.). Gift of Mrs. Samuel and Miss Alice Hooper. The Museum of Fine Arts, Boston.* After returning from Europe, Allston took considerable experimental risks in this portrayal of the prophet being fed miraculously by ravens in the wilderness. The lone human figure in the foreground is subservient to the picture's landscape elements: an encircling cavern of dark clouds and a twisted dead tree with tangled roots appearing to assume human form.

CHAPTER ONE

OUR OWN BRIGHT LAND

Thine eyes shall see the light of distant skies; Yet Cole! thy heart shall bear to Europe's strand
A living image of our own bright land, Such as upon thy glorious canvas lies.
—WILLIAM CULLEN BRYANT (from "To Cole, The Painter, Departing for Europe," 1829)

The vast array of artists whose work has come to be associated with the Hudson River School were only to varying degrees nativists in their outlook. Most of the painters who contributed to the movement acknowledged, at least in the temperament of their pictures, the English thinker and statesman Edmund Burke's association of the sublime with an "astonishment" in which all of the soul's "motions are suspended, with some degree of horror."

Given their religious presuppositions and insistence that American scenery should produce art morally superior to that of the Old World, many critics were more comfortable with John Ruskin's definition: "Sublimity is . . . another word for the effect of greatness upon the feelings." While Ruskin's mid-century work *Modern Painters* disparaged Claude Lorrain and exalted England's brilliant Joseph Mallord William Turner, Thomas Cole praised Claude and called Turner "one of the greatest Landscape painters that ever lived."

Cole's stroke of originality was to magnify the visually dramatic possibilities of landscape by communicating his deeply felt personal response to his subject. As early as 1828, *The Garden of Eden* and *The Expulsion from the Garden Eden* demonstrate Cole's fascination with stark categories of creation and apocalypse, paradise and banishment. Well before the overtly allegorical *The Course of Empire,* there is in these paintings a sense of parable that seems to animate the trees, geologic tumble, and the spray of the falls and rivers. This underlying murmuring—present even in Cole's purest landscapes—causes contemporary reviewers to respond with words like "homily."

Prior to 1825, the year marking the beginning of Cole's investigations of the Catskills and the Hudson

Expulsion from the Garden of Eden

THOMAS COLE. *c. 1827-1828; oil on canvas; 39 x 54 in. (99 x 137 cm). Gift of Mrs. Maxim Karolik for the M. and M. Karolik Collection of American Paintings, 1815-1865. The Museum of Fine Arts, Boston.* This landscape transcends portrayal of an earthly place and simultaneously incorporates detailed study of nature into a larger allegorical conception. The blazing light of God's command divides the picture in half: a sunlit paradise on the right, desolation and darkness on the left. Cole has included a gnarled tree in the left foreground.

The Titan's Goblet

THOMAS COLE. *1833; detail. Metropolitan Museum of Art. Gift of Samuel Avery, Jr., 1904.* No other work by Cole so boldly subordinates landscape elements to the imagination as does this cryptic vision. The goblet's basin and tree-encrusted rim, with boats and buildings, suggest a microcosm of the coast on which the gigantic artifact has been placed by some ancient, unseen hand. Uncharacteristically lacking in detail, the mountain range forms a strangely flat backdrop.

In Nature's Wonderland

THOMAS DOUGHTY. *1835; oil on canvas; 24 1/4 x 30 in. (62 x 76 cm). The Detroit Institute of Arts. Founders Society of Purchase, Gibbs-Williams Fund.* Doughty's remarkably tranquil "wonderland" is a composite of elements favored by Hudson River School painting. Delicately rendered flowers and trees draw the viewer past a promontory of rock into a pale infinity accentuated by pink clouds. The tiny viewer within the landscape is placed humbly at ground level near the central body of water.

The Course of Empire: The Savage State

THOMAS COLE. *1836; oil on canvas; 39 1/4 x 63 1/4 in. (100 x 161 cm). The New York Historical Society.* The first of the five landscapes with which Cole chose to construct an apocalyptic social allegory, this painting is already full of foreboding. The land, though primeval and unspoiled, is no Eden. Smoke rises from a colony of teepees while a hunter grimly pursues a stag in the foreground.

River, the art of landscape painting had fallen into neglect in America. After all, Sir Joshua Reynolds, the renowned portraitist, had authoritatively ranked it, in his *Discourses,* far from the pinnacle of artistic forms. The American artists who nevertheless quietly cultivated the form had a decisive impact on the young and as yet unknown Cole. One such painter was Thomas Doughty.

America's Revival of the Landscape

Doughty was born in Philadelphia in 1793. Self-taught, Doughty made his first serious attempts at landscape painting when he was twenty-seven, after what had already been a checkered career. *Autumn Scene on the Hudson* and *River Glimpse* date from the period of 1820–1821, and both demonstrate the painter's struggle with technical difficulties.

By 1822, however, his careful, locally based pictures were on display at the Philadelphia Academy of the Fine Arts, which had been chartered in 1806. Though not as intuitively and avowedly Claudian as the later proponent of Italianate landscape George Loring Brown (1814–1889), Doughty suffused his pictures in a similar lambency. These compositions were frequently assembled from elements from various locales that the artist found particularly striking. His principal motivation was to bring local scenery into focus and advance the worthiness of the rustic environment at hand for artistic perception. Doughty became the nation's first professional painter to make landscape his entire stock in trade.

The Course of Empire: Desolation

THOMAS COLE. *1836; oil on canvas; 39 1/4 x 63 1/4 in. (100 x 160 cm). New York Historical Society.* Preceded by *The Savage State, The Consummation of Empire,* and *Destruction,* the final, almost surrealist, canvas in Cole's series shows a civilization in ruins, having succumbed to inevitable violence and corruption. Cole's studies in Europe are reflected not only in his theory of history but in the Corinthian column, which now supports only a bird's nest.

Also at the Philadelphia exhibit were the landscapes of Thomas Birch, a student of Thomas Sully and John Wesley Jarvis. Birch, best known for his marine paintings, was an English immigrant who had worked in Philadelphia with his father engraving and publishing views of the city. He, Sully, and Jarvis had undertaken a trip along the Schuylkill River, sketching diligently as they traveled.

In 1823, having trekked through Ohio and Pennsylvania painting views of the countryside rather than portraits of the sitters he had hoped for, an itinerant Thomas Cole found Doughty and Birch's view paintings hanging in the academy. The combination of skill and devotion he saw in their efforts not only amazed him but galvanized his objectives as an artist. He had discovered what he later called "the standard by which I form

River View with Hunters and Dogs

THOMAS DOUGHTY, *c. 1850; oil on canvas; 18 3/4 x 25 in. (47 x 64 cm).*
National Museum of American Art, Washington, D. C.
Painted roughly twenty-five years after Doughty set out to turn local scenery into landscape art, this placid river view with gently rolling mountains in the distance shows that his earlier tightness of brushstroke has relaxed. Careful Claudian arrangement of a flat rock and a clump of trees in the foreground brings the eye to the picture's center, where a hunter walks with his dogs.

In Nature's Wonderland

THOMAS DOUGHTY. *1835; detail. The Detroit Institute of*
the Arts. Founders Society of Purchase, Gibbs-Williams Fund.
Doughty's pioneering interest in local scenery was to remain true to a quietly contemplative Romanticism and reverence for nature. Rendered in muted blues, greens, and browns, the cliff contrasts with the mild glow of the misty sky—a composition that seems to anticipate the Luminism of Kensett and Gifford

Moonlit Landscape

WASHINGTON ALLSTON. *1819;*
oil on canvas; 24 x 35 in. (61 x 89 cm).
The Museum of Fine Arts, Boston.
Gift of William of William Sturgis Bigelow.
A well-known example of Allston's deter-
mined Romanticism, this view demonstrates the painter's dreamlike blurring
of definition, similar to the murky effects
associated with Albert Pinkham Ryder.
Under the cold eye of a brilliant moon,
Allston has placed a river traversed by a
bridge, a beached boat, and an encounter
among four figures, one on horseback.

my judgment." Some scholars have found Doughty's achievements substantial enough to
merit considering him on a par with Cole himself as a cofounder of the American landscape enterprise of the 1820s.

The Effect of Tourism

Eighteenth-century America had proven peculiarly indifferent to the issue of the picturesque, evincing little interest in the concept of art as a reflection of American natural
splendor. The capability—that is, the necessary leisure and education—for appreciation
of wilderness as art was confined to a small gentry.

When a sizable urban elite and middle class began to come into their own during the
early nineteenth century, tourism soon followed. People sought out pleasure and recre-
ation through sightseeing in a domestic near-abroad as well as in Europe. The touristic
venture, the pursuit of leisure through travel, and the cosmopolitan experience had intellectual consequences. American perceptions of the homeland began to shift. The possi-
bility for objectifying a view for the sake of art had begun to take hold. A natural site could
be recontextualized. It could be drawn.

From 1820 to 1821, *Picturesque Views of American Scenery* was published in Philadelphia,
with the drawings of Joshua Shaw engraved by John Hill. Aquatints done by Hill of drawings by the Englishman William Guy Wall graced the pages of *Hudson River Portfolio,*
which was published in New York in 1827. By 1830 Thomas Doughty had begun pub-

lishing his *Cabinet of Natural History and American Rural Sports,* featuring Doughty's own hand-tinted lithographs. *American Scenery,* probably the best-known tourist guide of its kind, was published in 1840 and included William Henry Bartlett's engravings of the Catskills, the Hudson River, and the Connecticut River Valley.

In the 1820s, the period of Cole and Doughty's explorations, most depictions of various tourist sites fell into two categories: the merely picturesque and the morally earnest. One was intended to advertise tourism, concentrating, in many cases, on depicting what today might be called the educated consumer. The other equated the art of landscape with moral utility. Viewing a location that became part of the early Hudson River School legend, Kaaterskill Falls, one tourist recounted his impression with almost textbook piety. He wrote that it "makes a man feel like a poor worm, or elevates him to a sublimity in keeping with his own, as his humility or his pride is uppermost."

In addition to Kaaterskill Clove, which Cole had documented on canvas in 1826, and where Asher Durand situated his reverential portrayal of the painter with the poet Bryant, tourists and artists visited Mount Washington, Trenton Falls, and the Great Falls of the Potomac. Niagara Falls, however, summed up, in its roar and immense scale, the essence of what could be called sublime imagery in the American east of Cole's time. It was, according to Cole, "[a] wonder of the world."

Cole's account of the impression Niagara made on him during a visit in 1829 leaves little doubt that his understanding of the sublime coincided with that of Edmund Burke: he compared the falls to Dante's *Inferno*, "to waters of the infernal regions" that took on "a dreadful and terrifying character." Its unsurpassed significance to painters ranging from Frederic Edwin Church and Jasper Francis Cropsey to John Frederick Kensett and Albert

The Finding of Moses
Salvator Rosa. *1660-1665; oil on canvas; 48 1/4 x 80 in. (123 x 203 cm). Detroit Institute of Arts. Gift of Mr. and Mrs. Edgar B. Whitcomb.* When Cole and other Hudson River School painters traveled to Europe, study of Salvator (1615-1673) and Claude was considered essential. Salvator has framed the infant Moses, the Pharaoh's daughter, and her servants with an arch of rocks, windblown trees, and billowing clouds. Nature appears to brood over the portentous implications of this biblical event.

Bierstadt makes Niagara a visual event that unifies and defines the expansive Hudson River School.

While Niagara was a natural formation too grand and sensational to ignore for followers of Cole, the Connecticut River Valley's Mount Holyoke represented a central technical and aesthetic breakthrough for American landscape art. What became the all-purpose strategy of the panorama originated in Cole's sizing up of the formidable problem posed by the view from Mount Holyoke. Measuring 1,070 feet in height on the Connecticut River, Holyoke was already a landmark in the American tourist trade, having been an attraction since 1821.

Following page:
The Oxbow
(The Connecticut River near Northampton)
THOMAS COLE. *1836; oil on canvas; 51 1/2 x 76 in. (131 x 193 cm).*
Metropolitan Museum of Art, New York. Gift of Mrs. Russell Sage,
1908. Planning an unusual landscape to show at the National
Academy of Art, Cole wrote in 1836: "I have already com-
menced a view from Mt. Holyoke ... it will be novel and
I think effective." Ignoring prevailing orthodoxy against
"long views," Cole managed to bend this mountaintop
scene into a panorama that combines depth and rich detail.

Early Morning at Cold Spring

ASHER BROWN DURAND. *1850; oil on canvas; 59 x 47 1/2 in.*
(150 x 121 cm). Montclair Art Museum, New Jersey, Lang Acquisition
Fund, 1945. Durand's landscape has more in common with
Doughty's quiet encounters with nature than with Cole's more
theatrical style. The unassuming figure standing beside a row of
trees contemplates the scene before him. He, like the viewer, is a
spectator of the landscape. The village is a benign adjunct to nature.

Leatherstocking Meets the Law

JOHN QUIDOR. *1832; oil on canvas; 10 1/8 x 13 1/4 in. (28 x 34 cm).*
New York State Historical Association, Cooperstown. By lending his almost
satirical style to picturing the Hudson River Valley characters of Irving
and Cooper, Quidor brought attention to local society and scenery.
His depiction of Cooper's frontiersman-hero, Leatherstocking, flintlock
in hand, shows the comedic side of Quidor's sense of the grotesque.
The scene's mountains and trees are distorted through his pictorial lens.

The European Imperative

American tourism in Europe, principally in Italy and England, was, at first, restricted primarily to America's intelligentsia, but for American painters, whether well-to-do or down at the heel, crossing the Atlantic was a necessary pilgrimage. Cole journeyed to Europe twice. The first visit lasted from 1829 to 1832, with sixteen months spent in Italy, the second, from 1841 to 1842. Bryant's admonitions were probably unnecessary. In a letter from Florence, written while working on "a view of the Campagna of Rome—broken aqueducts, etc.," Cole noted, "But I long for the wild mountains of the West."

Martin Johnson Heade, the most startlingly enigmatic contributor to the mysterious, highly Romantic body of work called Luminism, ventured to England, France, and Italy in 1837. He ended up in Rome, where he remained until 1839. Asher Brown Durand, joined by his American colleagues John W. Casilear, T. P. Rossiter, and John Frederick Kensett, departed for Europe in 1840 to study for a year. Although his pockets were not as deep as his friends', Kensett's tour was a grand one, lasting seven years and taking him to England, France, Italy, and Germany.

The Titan's Goblet
THOMAS COLE. *1833; oil on canvas; 19 3/8 x 16 1/8 in. (49 x 41 cm). Metropolitan Museum of Art, New York. Gift of Samuel Avery, Jr., 1904.* With this picture, Cole achieved perhaps his most succinct allegorical image while creating an enduring oddity of American painting. The goblet atop the cliff, filled to the brim, its stem treelike and covered with vegetation, may refer to Teutonic mythology's prehuman giants. The community below seems indifferent to its presence. Another civilization inhabits the goblet itself.

Raftsmen Playing Cards
GEORGE CALEB BINGHAM. *1847-1850; oil on canvas; 28 x 38 in. (71 x 97 cm). The St. Louis Art Museum. Ezra E. Linley Fund.* Bingham focused on Missourians who worked on the rivers and even politicians on the stump. Unlike Cole's human figures, which seem wooden and subordinate to larger themes, Bingham's cardplayers are depicted realistically and sympathetically. The river, river banks, and hot overcast sky show Bingham had much in common with the Luminists.

Catskill, New York

ALBURTIUS DEL ORIENT BROWERE. *1849; oil on canvas; 34 x 4 1/4 in. (86 x 12 cm). The Brooklyn Museum, Dick S. Ramsay Fund.* Born in Tarrytown, New York, Browere (1814-1887) spent most of his life in New York City but journeyed twice to California as a gold prospector. This expansive and airy view of Catskill, the town where Cole made his home, features an intimate view of a house and a sailboat on the river. Its evenly diffused light and minimal foreground are consistent with Luminism.

The year of Kensett's return to America, immediately preceding Europe's revolutionary convulsion of 1848, saw George Inness travel there, one of several visits by the painter from Newburgh, New York. James Hamilton, the Irish-born "American Turner," returned from Europe in 1855, having spent a year studying—not surprisingly—the English genius whose work awakened his fascination with the sea. Jasper Francis Cropsey, too, sailed for Europe in 1856, settling in London until 1863.

Whig politician and socially observant painter of his native Missouri, George Caleb Bingham received his most important training in Düsseldorf from 1856 to 1858. Also to roam Europe were artists whose initiation as landscape painters began on the Eastern seaboard but who developed a monumental Western idiom as they followed westward expansion beyond the Mississippi into the plains and Rocky Mountains. Albert Bierstadt, who arrived in America with his family while a child in 1832, returned in 1853 to Germany—to Düsseldorf—not far from his birthplace, Solingen. Four years earlier Worthington Whittredge had gone to Rome and Düsseldorf, where he became acquainted with Bierstadt before moving on to Switzerland and Italy in1854. In 1855, Sanford R. Gifford began a three-year course of study on the Continent. Thomas Moran, accompanied by his brother Edward, also made Turner the focus of his studies while in England in 1862.

Cole and Durand Discover America

The turning point for Thomas Cole and for American painting was the artist's trip up the Hudson River, four years before his visit to Europe. Rather than Cole's unself-conscious Romanticism, it was the object itself—the wholehearted affirmation of the environment—that asserted a uniquely American content within a coherent framework: the landscape.

In 1825 three distinguished gentlemen happened upon Cole's work in a New York frame shop. One was John Trumbull, former student of Benjamin West's, founder of the American Academy of the Fine Arts in New York and neoclassical painter of scenes from the Revolutionary War, in which he had served with the Continental Army. The others were the critic William Dunlap and the young engraver and portrait painter Asher Brown Durand, who, in 1823, established his reputation with an engraving of Trumbull's *Declaration of Independence.*

Cole's work was an immediate hit with these three discerning observers. The unknown artist's pictures managed to meet Dunlap's severe criteria, which he once put this way: "That painter is good for nothing who cannot impress us with the moral sublimity of virtue, and give us the majesty of religion with all her sweetness." Much of Dunlap's definition of virtue had to do with being the friend of reason, truth, and religion. As for the element of truth, Cole had shown to Dunlap's satisfaction that "every ramification and twig was studied." The self-centered Trumbull, who had tried his hand at an unmemorable *View of Niagara Falls,* praised Cole obliquely: "This youth has done what I have attempted in vain."

Durand would go on to become the chief exponent of a theology of American landscape based on Cole's achievement. But Durand's discipleship apparently did not include unwa-

**Scene on the Hudson
(Rip Van Winkle)**
JAMES HAMILTON. *1845; oil on canvas; 38 1/8 x 57 1/8 in. (97 x 145 cm). National Museum of American Art, Smithsonian Institution.*
Hamilton (1819-1878) painted this pleasing view along the Hudson a decade before traveling to England to study the extraordinary work of J. M. W. Turner, which he sought to imitate. This landscape includes Irving's famed character but on a scale reminiscent of Cole's small human figures. The trees in the foreground are rendered with Durand-like care.

**View of Schroon
Mountain, Essex
County, New York,
After a Storm**
THOMAS COLE.
*1838; oil on canvas;
39 1/2 x 63 1/2 in.
(100 x 161 cm). The
Cleveland Museum of Art.
The Hinman B. Hurlbut
Collection, (1335.17).*
This study of a mountain
exemplifies Cole's more
naturalistic mode, without
narrative interference.
While the Schroon aims
upward at a patch of blue,
another hill covered with
a blanket of brilliant reds,
yellows, and greens slopes
downward from the right,
where the storm has
drifted. Closer up stand
two trees, one still green,
the other almost bare.

The Storm

GEORGE CALEB BINGHAM, *c. 1852-1853;*
oil on canvas; 25 x 30 1/16 in. (64 x 76 cm).
Wadsworth Atheneum, Hartford,
Connecticut. Gift of Henry E. Schnakenberg.
Although Bingham is best known as
a genre painter and popularizer of life
along the Mississippi and Missouri
rivers, he brought to the frontier a
concern for native landscape. This
depiction of a mountain forest interior
during a storm, with its running deer and
brilliantly lit splintered tree, shows his
admiration for German Romantic style.

vering allegiance to the doctrine of self-expression that Cole had made clear in a heated exchange with Baltimore art patron Robert Gilmor, Jr. To Cole, simple imitation of nature was inadequate; to Durand, it was something of an ideal.

Durand was born in 1796 in Jefferson Village, New Jersey, at the foot of the Orange Mountain. His grandfather, Jean Durand, a Huguenot, had fled to England to escape the French monarchy's persecution of Protestants, eventually settling in Milford, Connecticut. Durand's father, a watchmaker, was born there in 1745. Something of a boy naturalist, Durand spent much of his time exploring the nearby mountain and would, according to his own description, "hide behind a tree or bush at the approach of a person or vehicle." In 1812 Durand obtained an apprenticeship with the nation's leading engraver, Peter Maverick, in New York. Five years later, Durand was Maverick's partner, but professional rivalry eventually drove a wedge between the two.

Soon the signature, "Engraved by Durand," became connected with prominent names in American art: Vanderlyn (*Ariadne*) and Allston (*Spalatro and the Bloody Hand*) as well as Trumbull. Making engravings for Cooper's novel *The Spy* (1821) may have also reinforced whatever Durand knew of Romanticism through his exposure to

The Tornado

THOMAS COLE. *1835; oil on canvas;*
46 3/8 x 64 5/8 in. (118x164 cm).
The Collection of the Corcoran Gallery
of Art, Museum Purchase, Gallery Fund.
Cole's concept of the sublime
reaches cyclonic force in this picture.
The astonishment and horror
stressed in Edmund Burke's theory
of the sublime is given full reign
as Cole's tornado blackens earth
and sky. Lit dimly from above and
along the horizon, this mysterious
scene of natural destruction is
dominated by three shattered trees.

Allston's work. By 1830 his finest plates were increasingly appreciations of landscapes by Doughty and Cole.

That year Durand planned to publish a series titled *The American Landscape* that was to include engravings of his own paintings and text by William Cullen Bryant. The project was discontinued when the engraver discovered that his finest efforts so far were a marketing flop. Having first won recognition after three years' work on Trumbull's epic painting, his impressive catalogue of accomplishments as an engraver threatened to scupper his ambitions as a painter.

The renowned patron of the arts Luman Reed, who financed Cole's five-picture series *The Course of Empire,* rescued Durand from the "background" to which one critic was quick to relegate him in 1830. Commissions from Reed enabled Durand to make the transition from engraver to full-time landscape painter. Cole and Durand became regular correspondents, and by 1836, the year of Reed's death, Cole wrote to Durand: "I am pleased that you have attacked a landscape, and have no doubt that you will succeed to the satisfaction of all except yourself." In 1837 Cole took Durand on a tour of the Catskills, much of which Durand had never seen. Cole made a point of showing him prized locations rather than hoarding them as exclusive objects of inspiration.

Rising to become president of the National Academy of Design in 1845, a vital institution he and Cole founded in 1826, Durand began to help steer the American landscape in the direction of a narrow orthodoxy. His influence no doubt made itself felt through New

York's Century Association, which he joined as a charter member in 1847.

Unlike Cole, whose pictures were often composites of pure invention and studies from nature, Durand stood for direct reporting, or imitation, of the scene. This would lead to a method of painting that was entirely at the mercy of a view's complexities. Regard for composition and for what other artists had done before was secondary to declaring "the glory of God, by a representation of his works, and not the works of man. . . . It is only thus you can learn to read the great book of Nature . . . and attach to the transcript your own commentaries." The self-expressive force in Cole's paintings, which plays itself out in a clash of poetical imagery and realistic representation, is not found in Durand's work.

Study from Nature: Rocks and Trees

Asher Brown Durand, c. 1836; oil on canvas; 21 1/2 x 17 in. (55 x 43 cm). Collection of The New York Historical Society. Durand once asked why the American landscape painter should not "boldly originate a high and independent style based on his native resources." Durand showed a degree of independence from Cole's more idealized landscape vision. His belief in transcribing forest scenes exactly as he found them led to several studies such as this one.

Kindred Spirits

Asher Brown Durand. 1849; oil on canvas; 46 x 36 in. (117 x 94 cm). The New York Public Library. Astor, Lenox, and Tilden Foundations. Perhaps Durand's best-known work, it is both landscape (of the Kaaterskill Clove) and portrait. Painted to commemorate Cole shortly after his death, it depicts the artist and poet William Cullen Bryant over-looking the near mythic haunt of the Hudson River School Durand's command of detail and dedication to the scene's elements are evident.

CHAPTER TWO

THE MOMENT OF AMERICAN LANDSCAPE

*The future spirit of our art must be
inherently vast like our western plains, majestic
like our forests, generous like our rivers.*
—Anonymous Critic, 1853

The 1840s and 1850s were a period of expansion and consolidation for the native school named for the Hudson River. Although without a convenient appellation at the time, the movement produced a generation of adventurer-explorer artists who would travel well beyond the White Mountains to the Rockies and the Andes of South America—all in order to advance the cause of American painting.

The American Transcendentalists' argument that bonding with nature's solitude and silence nurtured spiritual development and character could hardly have been discouraging to American landscapists. Beginning with Ralph Waldo Emerson's philosophy of the spiritual over the material, which had been fully stated by 1844, and Henry David Thoreau's claim for nature's superiority over civilization, new literary voices answered the call of

Niagara

Frederic Edwin Church. *1857; detail. In the Collection
of the Corcoran Gallery of Art, Washington, D.C. Museum
Purchase, Gallery Fund.* Church produced this astounding
documentation of the Horseshoe Fall and the edge of
Goat Island from sketches made in 1856 on the Canadian
side of the falls. A tremendous expenditure of detail
can be seen in every stage of the water's journey downward as well as in the optical flourish of the rainbow.

Irving, Cooper, and Bryant. Henry Wadsworth Longfellow and Nathaniel Hawthorne became interested in painters' endeavors. Although Transcendentalism exacted a price among painters in terms of individuality, it was not alien to the current of Romanticism underlying the burgeoning landscape aesthetic. In effect, landscapists enjoyed the continuity of support they first received in the 1820s from important American thinkers and writers.

New financial resources for artists also rolled into place with the creation in New York of the Apollo Association in 1839, which became in 1844 the American Art Union. Until its dissolution in 1852 by court order as an illegal lottery, the Art Union marketed culture to the masses and gained publicity and capital for native artists. It accomplished this by purchasing artists' work and then holding an annual raffle in which Art Union members, who had paid an eligibility fee, were able to win actual paintings.

Engravings of these paintings also were made available to Art Union subscribers. Thus thousands of households became familiar, for example, with George Caleb Bingham's antic Missouri cardplayers and boatmen. Fine art was becoming popular in the larger culture. The number of subscribers reached a peak of 16,000 in 1848 when Cole's *The Voyage of Life,* originally painted for Samuel Ward, became a prize in the Art Union's lottery. Members of the Art Union also were recipients of the art journals *Bulletin* and *Transactions,* which served to illuminate the role of art in American society and stimulate public dialogue on the topic.

Prompted by the Art Union's example, similar organizations quickly caught on in Boston, Cincinnati, and Philadelphia. The significance of this boosterism for American artists becomes apparent when the fact is taken into account that a system of galleries and sophisticated dealers was not yet in place during the 1840s. Once the Art Union was abolished, artists were once

again forced to rely on a few large annual exhibitions and sales out of their own studios. The suit that led to the Art Union's downfall began with mutterings of discontent from disgruntled painters who claimed not to have profited in their dealings with the institution. The actual instrument of recrimination, however, was the National Academy of Design, which brought the fatal court action against the Art Union.

Following page:
The Voyage of Life: Manhood
THOMAS COLE. *1842; oil on canvas; 52 7/8 x 79 1/4 in. (134 x 201 cm). Munson-Williams Proctor Institute, Utica, New York. The abundant wonders and optimism of the quiet lagoon are gone, replaced by rapids and jagged rocks. The Voyager, now middle-aged, is surrounded by darkness and has lost control of his boat, which appears headed toward destruction. He looks heavenward for help and, according to Cole, is saved by "a Superior Power."*

The Voyage of Life: Childhood
THOMAS COLE. *1842; oil on canvas; 52 7/8 x 77 7/8 in. (133 x 198 cm). Munson-Williams Proctor Institute, Utica, New York.* In 1836, following completion of the epic *The Course of Empire,* Cole planned his best-known work, choosing as its subject the nature of human life itself. Guided by an "Angelic Form," the infant "Voyager" in a boat emerges from a cave that represents, in Cole's words, "our earthly origin, the mysterious Past."

The Voyage of Life: Youth
Thomas Cole. *1842; oil on canvas; 52 7/8 x 76 1/4 in. (134 x 194 cm). Munson-Williams Proctor Institute, Utica, New York.* The child approaches adulthood. His boat, which resembles a leaf or seed pod, contains a miniature garden of its own. Its carved prow and sides represent "the Hours," according to Cole. With the angel watching from the shore, the Voyager now steers along the "Stream of Life." Nature is in full flower, and the clouds form a palace of youthful aspiration.

The Voyage of Life: Old Age

THOMAS COLE. *1842; oil on canvas; 52 1/2 x 77 1/4 in. (133 x 196 cm). Munson-Williams Proctor Institute, Utica, New York.* The transition from a scene of storm-tossed suspense to one of dreamlike stillness seems to be Cole's way of effectively evoking the sublime. The boat's prow, a winged female holding an hourglass, has been lost. As the angelic being approaches the old man, divine light signifying immortality breaks through roiling black clouds.

Cole's Student

In June 1844, four years before his death, Thomas Cole accepted his only student: Frederic Edwin Church, who, during his lifetime, would be apotheosized as America's greatest painter. Church became one of the nation's wealthiest artists, leaving, at his death in 1900, almost half a million dollars in securities (a huge sum for its time).

In the sense that he was the only American landscape painter to study directly with Cole—actually boarding at the master's home at Catskill until 1846—Church possessed indisputable credentials as a formulator of the Hudson River School. Church is also distinguished by the fact that unlike his contemporaries Kensett, Whittredge, and Gifford, he was reluctant to go to Europe and relatively impervious to the traditions of Rome, Florence, and Düsseldorf. He finally made the journey in 1869 but, in keeping with his flair for exoticism, also incorporated the Near East into his travels, journeying to Beirut, Jerusalem, Damascus, Constantinople (Istanbul), and the Black Sea.

The fact that Church's extraordinary work and career represent an aesthetic divergence from Cole's more mythic content seems to follow from his being, without any doubt, possessed of a remarkably independent vision. If not "the Michelangelo of Landscape Art" that some of his peers regarded him to be, Church easily impressed his famous teacher as having nothing less than "the finest eye for drawing in the world."

Church was born in 1826 in Hartford, Connecticut, into a family whose name led back to the settlement's Puritan founders. As unpromising as it must have seemed to his business-man father, Joseph, for Church to pursue a career in art (his mother, Eliza Janes, warned against "the pleasure of the world"), he was permitted to study under two local artists and then his parents had him introduced to Cole.

In 1849 the National Academy of Design (of which Church had been named its youngest member the previous year) exhibited the painter's *West Rock, New Haven*, the culmination of his sketching in the Berkshires, Catskills, Green Mountains, and throughout Connecticut. This rectangle already contained qualities that set Church apart from Cole's studies of somber heroism. His brush work coolheadedly recorded what he saw, showing none of Cole's more agitated style, and demonstrated what one viewer called "the accuracy of a daguerreotype."

Joseph Church never referred to his son's painting as anything but "business" and offered financial assistance only after Frederic began proving the profitability of his work. By 1850 Church, having moved to New York soon after completing his studies with Cole,

Rocks off Grand Manan

FREDERIC EDWIN CHURCH. *c. 1851-52; oil with graphite on composition board; 12 x 16 in. (31 x 41 cm). Gift of Louis P. Church.* Church studied with the more idealistic Cole—perhaps partly explaining his search for topographical grandeur in South America and the far north. This view off the coast of Canada's Grand Manan island demonstrates Church's facility at portraying geological formations and water but also provides evidence for his occasional association with Luminism.

found a buyer for three of his paintings: the American Art Union. The painter received the princely sum of a thousand dollars for his work. He also took a studio at the Art Union Building, and before its doors were finally closed, the Art Union had purchased twenty-nine of the artist's paintings. Some of these early works' titles thematically echo Cole, such as *The River of the Waters of Life* and *The Plague of Darkness*.

From Quito to Labrador

Church had made it the aim of his work to do nothing less than "embrace the universe"—a phrase of Emerson's he seemed to have adopted as a credo. Oddly, he was not one for theorizing, just as he was inclined to dismiss European academicism. However, his belief that nature itself was the artist's best teacher extends logically to his interest in the natural sciences, which presumably held a torch up to cosmic darkness.

John Ruskin's analysis of J. M. W. Turner, *Modern Painters*, cannot be underestimated with respect to Church's thinking, but it was Alexander von Humboldt's *Cosmos* that addressed Church's interest in the Earth, matter, and space. "Landscape painting," Humboldt wrote, "requires for its development a large number of various and direct impressions, which when received must be fertilized by the powers of the mind, in order to be given back to the senses of others as a free work of art."

Cotopaxi

Frederic Edwin Church. *1862; oil on canvas; 48 x 85 in. (122 x 216 cm). The Reading Public Museum, Reading, Pennsylvania.*
Church's interest in J. M. W. Turner's landscapes and images of cosmic grandeur seem to coalesce in this geologic epic, showing the erupting Ecuadorean volcano and, just beyond, the sun seeming to shower the molten terrain with fire. Church evokes a scientific vision of the Earth's development.

In 1852 the natural scientist's *Personal Narrative of Travels to the Equinoctial Regions of America* appeared, and, in 1853, Church was in Quito, Ecuador, living in the house occupied by Humboldt forty years earlier.

After exploring Ecuador again in 1857, Church produced in his New York studio statements of grandiloquent naturalism based on his South American sketches.

These works include *The Andes of Ecuador* (1855), *Cayambe* (1858), the volcanological *Cotopaxi* (1862), and *The Heart of the Andes* (1859). The latter painting received thunderous critical acclaim, wild adulation from the public, and brought the artist the then unprecedented sum of $10,000. It epitomized the sort of reception that the unveiling of a painting by Church could now be expected to ignite.

Although he had gone to South America in large part because European painters had not, thus aiming to capitalize on the Andean sublime, Church's greatest success was his *Niagara*, completed after returning from Ecuador. Built up in his studio from various sketches, its realism—or optical illusion—astounded and delighted Americans. John Ruskin viewed it in London and fully allowed his disbelief to be suspended.

West Rock, New Haven
FREDERIC EDWIN CHURCH. *1849;*
oil on canvas; 26 1/2 x 40 in. (67 x 102 cm).
New Britain Museum of American Art,
Connecticut, John Butler Talcott Fund.
One year after Cole's death, Church
was recognized by the National Academy
of Design as having leaped to the fore-
front of landscape painters with this
picture's exhibition. Church presents
the rural New England scene on a
grand scale, while his virtuoso realism
shines in the stream, the cumulus
clouds overhead, and in the rock itself.

Niagara

FREDERIC EDWIN CHURCH. *1857; oil on canvas; 42 1/2 x 90 1/2 in. (108 x 230 cm). Collection of The Corcoran Gallery of Art, Washington, D. C., Museum Purchase, Gallery Fund.* A view of Niagara Falls, a place one seventeenth-century French explorer called the "horrible precipice," was essential to any Hudson River School painter's commitment to the sublime in American scenery. Church assembled this tour de force of water effects from sketches in his studio. It assured Church near-legendary status in his lifetime.

"With the exception of an occasional vein, which is blue as sapphire, or stains from rock, an iceberg is purely white, an opaque, dead white," Church noted in 1859. His expedition to Labrador, accompanied by Louis Noble, Cole's biographer, was again a search for the new. By this time, Church deliberately played up the angle of great adventurer. Church's trip, however, proved to be not at all perilous. The painter collected

in drawings the various optical and light effect he observed in the icebergs and returned to New York as the nation teetered on the brink of civil war. *The Icebergs* was eventually purchased by an Englishman, Thomas Watson, in 1863.

Church kept in mind Turner's incomparable ability to capture light reflected on the sea and refracted in nebulous skies, but the result is overblown documenta-tion. Not every reviewer gushed over his accomplishments. James Jackson Jarves, criti-cal nemesis of Church and Bierstadt, wrote in 1864: "Church's pictures have no reserved power of suggestion, but expand their force in coup-de-main effects. Hence it is that specta-tors are so loud in their exclamations of delight."

The Coming Storm
MARTIN JOHNSON HEADE. *1859; oil on canvas; 28 x 44 in. (71 x 111 an.). Metropolitan Museum of Art, Gift of Erving Wolf Foundation and Mr. and Mrs. Erving Wolf, 1975, (1975. 160).* Suspenseful moments before coastal storms inspired Heade's most otherworldly visions. The rapidly changing light falls on a man and dog calmly watching at the edge of the black, glassy water as a white-shirted rower ventures into the darkness. The illuminated shore-line curves toward the sailboat in the center.

The Luminist

In 1866, greeted by no ringing applause or fanfare, Martin Johnson Heade returned from Nicaragua to New York, where he sublet Church's studio space at the Tenth Street Building. Designed by the painter William Morris Hunt and constructed in 1857, the building became a haven for both the underrated and acclaimed among American artists, including Bierstadt, Gifford, Whittredge, John La Farge, Eastman Johnson, and Winslow Homer.

Here Heade lived and worked, off and on, until 1881. He ventured initially to Brazil in 1863, attracted to South America, like his friend Church, by its remote wonders but also, coincidentally, in a scientific connection. Heade's object of study, however, was zoological rather than geological. At the suggestion of a naturalist, J. C. Fletcher, the artist went to Brazil to illustrate a book on South American hummingbirds.

A glance at *Cattleya Orchid and Three Brazilian Hummingbirds* (1871) reveals Heade's originality. Nothing like John James Audubon's linear anatomical studies of North American species, Heade's hummingbirds seem to float within a softly glowing tropical forest. For all its subtlety, the light achieved by this artist's paintings has a spellbinding power.

Heade's concentration during the late 1860s on advancing and retreating thunderstorms in the marshlands of coastal New England has increasingly come to define Luminism. Since 1943, when his Rhode Island squalls and shorelines were rediscovered—most notably, the cryptic *Thunder Storm on Narragansett*

Thunder Storm on Narragansett Bay

MARTIN JOHNSON HEADE. *1868; oil on canvas; 32 1/8 x 54 1/2 in. (82 x 138 cm). Amon Carter Museum, Fort Worth, Texas.* Of Heade's intensely imagined thunderstorm paintings, none surpasses this impenetrable enigma. The sky consists of two horizontal bands, one black, the other gray. As the storm sweeps the horizon, two strangely radiant sailboats are mirrored in the glistening, black waters. While a thread of lightning zigzags in the distance, two unconcerned figures stroll onto the luminous shore.

Approaching Storm: Beach Near Newport

MARTIN JOHNSON HEADE. *c. 1867; oil on canvas; 28 x 58 1/4 in. (71 x 148 cm). The Museum of Fine Arts, Boston. Gift of Mrs. Maxim Karolik for the M. and M. Karolik Collection of American Paintings, 1815-1865.* Though not devoted to the marine form, Heade seemed to have perfected his startling Luminist technique with his scenes of coastal storms. His expressive force is uncompromising in the feathery stippling of the waves that stands out against the deep-green sea and in the crescent-shaped shoreline caught, here and there, in mysterious spotlight effects.

**Owl's Head,
Penobscot Bay, Maine**
FITZ HUGH LANE. *1862;
oil on canvas; 16 x 26 in.
(41 x 66 cm). Museum of Fine
Arts, Boston. Bequest of Martha
C. Karolik for the M. and M.
Karolik Collection of American
Paintings, 1815-1865.*
A marine painter from
Gloucester, Massachusetts,
Lane (1804-1865) furthered his
experimentation with light in
views of coastal New England
from 1848 until his death.
Schooners often figured promi-
nently in his work, but in this
late coastal view, the founder of
Luminism has understated the
sailboat in the bay and flooded
the picture with gentle light.

**The Narrows
from Staten Island**
JASPER FRANCIS CROPSEY.
*1866-1868; 42 x 72 1/8 in.
(107 x 183 cm). Amon Carter
Museum, Fort Worth, Texas.
Acquisition in memory of Richard
Fargo Brown, Trustee, Amon
Carter Museum, 1961-1972.*
A contemporary of Kensett,
Gifford, and Church, Cropsey
(1823-1900) painted numerous
charming, but generally unex-
ceptional, views of Niagara
Falls and the Catskills. This
remarkable panorama, with
rich land and marine textures,
was planned in 1863, but,
when exhibited, was
already out of fashion.

Brace's Rock, Brace's Cove
FITZ HUGH LANE. *1864; detail. Daniel J. Terra Collection. Terra Museum of American Art, Chicago.*
Often inviting comparisons with surrealism and abstraction, this picture's striking qualities
of flatness, compactness of form, and emphasis on stark contrast heighten an impression
of unrelated objects in space. The symbolically charged boat Lane placed in the foreground
stands out against the tranquil cove and the tawny rock dominating the background.

**Brace's Rock,
Brace's Cove**

FITZ HUGH LANE. *1864;
oil on canvas; 10 1/4 x 15 1/4 in.
(26 x 39 cm). Daniel J. Terra
Collection, 3. 1983. Photograph
© 1995 Courtesy of Terra Museum
of American Art, Chicago.*
This painting's flat horizontal
composition, with barely any
foreground, and its pared-
down elements make one of
Luminism's most eloquent
statements. Black rocks contrast
with the lambent sky and faintly
rippling water. The wrecked
boat, a prop used also by
Heade, has been called an
allusion to the Civil War crisis.

Study of a Wood Interior

ASHER BROWN DURAND. *c. 1850; oil on canvas;
17 x 24 in. (43 x 70 cm). Addison Gallery of
American Art, Phillips Academy, Andover,
Massachusetts. Gift of Mrs. Frederic F. Durand.*
Durand's landscape vision was site specific
and sought not to meddle with the pictorial
jumble nature frequently offered up. This
view shows Durand at his most documen-
tary, yet concentration on the mossy
rocks lends the picture an almost abstract
quality. The woods are softly out of focus.

The Beeches

ASHER BROWN DURAND. *1845; oil on
canvas; 60 3/8 x 48 1/8 in. (153 x 122 cm).
Metropolitan Museum of Art, Bequest of
Maria DeWitt Jesup, from the collection of
her husband, Morris K. Jesup. (15.30.59).*
Durand's idyll is dominated by the foreground's arching trees, which allow only a
portion of the sky to be visible. As in *Early
Morning at Cold Spring,* a church steeple rises
in the distance—a footnote to the painter's
concern for the divine in nature. Following
the shepherd's progress, the viewer may not
notice the stumps of chopped-down trees.

Bay (1868)—Heade's work has invited speculation and defied neat interpretations.

Luminism itself was a term invented in 1954 to come to grips with an effect that shows up consistently in the work of New England seascapist Fitz Hugh Lane—considered to be its creator—as well as Heade's paintings and the coastal scenes of Francis A. Silva and Alfred Thompson Bricher. With its emphasis on smooth, seamless surfaces of light, Luminism is also generally considered to be the appropriate label for much of the work of Gifford and Kensett.

John Frederick Kensett:
Simplicity of Strength and Knowledge

Having left behind his job as an engraver with the American Bank Note Company of New York to go to Europe with Durand, Casilear, and Rossiter, Kensett entered the following fragment in his journal in 1840: "From the simplicity of indigence and ignorance to the simplicity of strength and knowledge." Beginning with his first canvases marked by admiration for Durand's methods to his later, ever more spare studies of form,

light, and space, Kensett seemed to have achieved his goal. Three years before finances allowed him to return home, he wanted "to get amid the scenery" of his own country "for it abounds with the picturesque, the grand, and the beautiful."

Born in Cheshire, Connecticut, in 1816, Kensett also traveled widely in America before his death in New York in December of 1872. His landscapes recorded unembellished scenes of the east in the Adirondacks, Catskills, White Mountains, and the Hudson but also looked westward, producing *Upper Mississippi* (1855), which prefigured elements of his later work, and the untypically dramatic *Storm, Western Colorado* (1870).

Once back in America, recognition was not to elude Kensett. In 1848, at the National Academy of Design, he showed the imagined—and pointedly Romantic—view titled *The Shrine—A Scene in Italy* and proved his mettle. Like Durand, however, Kensett preferred to paint specific sites. He shared with Cole a belief in landscape's moral dimension, but did not see humanity in collision with nature, nor did he portray human figures doing anything out of the ordinary in the outdoors. People were

Coast Scene with Figures
JOHN FREDERICK KENSETT. *1869; oil on canvas; 36 1/2 x 60 1/4 in. (92 x 153 cm). Wadsworth Atheneum, Hartford, Connecticut. Ella Gallup Sumner and Mary Catlin Sumner Collection.*
Kensett, like Durand, esteemed many seventeenth-century Dutch painters, including Jacob van Ruysdael, Willem van de Velde, and Meindert Hobbema. In this characteristic late Luminist work, Kensett may have had them in mind, especially with regard to the two figures on the beach as well as in the tightly painted waves.

harmonious participants in nature, neither hostile intruders nor players in a faraway drama.

Kensett's careful study of Claude is reflected in the serene composition of *The White Mountains—From North Conway* (1851). Composed almost entirely of Claudian devices, the painting enables the viewer to look downward, through the quiet and modest village, into a verdant pasture below Mount Washington. An ax has not been taken to a single tree. Even comparable landscapes from this period by Jasper F. Cropsey tended to suggest a border between civilization and nature.

A contemporary of Church and Bierstadt, Kensett stood almost at antipodes with them by painting in a style that was at first mindful of Cole and Durand but would continue to avoid bombast and sensation-

Eaton's Neck, Long Island
JOHN FREDERICK KENSETT. *1872; oil on canvas; 18 x 36 in. (46 x 91 cm). Metropolitan Museum of Art, New York, Gift of Thomas Kensett, 1874, (74.29).*
Kensett's highly innovative series, Last Summer's Work, done the year of his death, show the painter taking Luminism's logic of reduction to its minimalist conclusion. This painting conjoins four basic parts. With the metallic sky mirroring the flattened ocean, the Long Island beach and headland arc outward, almost meeting the horizon.

Following Page:
Lake George
JOHN FREDERICK KENSETT. *1869; oil on canvas; 44 1/8 x 66 3/8 in. (112 x 170 cm). Metropolitan Museum of Art, Bequest of Maria DeWitt Jesup, 1915, (15.30.61).* Also a subject, in 1862, for Martin Johnson Heade's more foreboding mood, this lake in the Adirondack mountains had been of interest to Kensett since 1853. Unlike Heade's vivid, otherworldly contrasts, Kensett preserves a sense of nature's stillness with the mono-chromatic light and gently rendered gray-green island masses strewn across the lake.

alism. Though frequently relying on large canvases, the painter filled them with unobtrusive and simplified pastoral grace, reaching a rarefied tranquility in the Last Summer's Work (1872). This series, focusing on coastal scenes in New England and Long Island, shows that, at the end of his life, Kensett was approaching a compression and reduction that could only solidify his association with Luminism.

Although critics in Kensett's lifetime, including Henry Tuckerman and Jarves, found his work difficult to classify, they also found in it almost nothing to dislike. Jarves considered him "more refined in sentiment" than his two showman-like peers. Tuckerman praised him for being "often the most satisfactory." One member of the Century Club wrote elegiacally that Kensett "became a classic among our artists, free from all the prevailing or tempting excesses."

Along the Hudson
JOHN FREDERICK KENSETT. *1852; oil on canvas; 18 1/8 x 24 in. (46 x 61 cm). National Museum of American Art, Smithsonian Institution. Bequest of Helen Huntington Hull.* Profoundly influenced by Claude while in Europe and by Durand in America, Kensett, unlike Cole, preferred specific sites and carried no allegorical baggage. This Luminist river view is broken into a triangle of trees and rocks and a smooth field of pale, misty light.

Coast Scene with Figures
JOHN FREDERICK KENSETT. *1869; detail. Wadsworth Athenaeum, Hartford, Connecticut. Ella Gallup Sumner and Mary Catlin Sumner Collection.* Kensett found much in the New England shore that was compatible with his Luminist celebration of space and light. While Kensett's design is largely devoted to the creamy sky and the ocean's vastness and constancy, it also takes the rock and trees into careful account. The couple on this Massachusetts beach seem to convey a universal experience of awe.

CHAPTER THREE

A LAST GLIMPSE OF THE FRONTIER

*I have hoped to see the great artist, the strong man, overtopping in strength
the artists of any country, an American by birth. I have been so anxious to see him that
I have strained my eyes and wondered if that were not he in the distance.*
—WORTHINGTON WHITTREDGE

Beginning in 1859, when Albert Bierstadt set out to blaze a trail into the West with Colonel Frederick William Lander's Rocky Mountain expedition, the Hudson River ethos and its concept of the new was on a journey to an abyss made visible in 1875. Lander was looking for a way through the Rockies to the Far West and Pacific. Bierstadt was searching for new scenery, new wonders for epic-scale canvases.

The artist traveled with the army surveyors along the North Platte River only up to a point before finding the Wind River and Shoshone Mountains in the Nebraska Territory worthy of sketches and photographs. His colleagues from his European period in Düsseldorf and Italy, Sanford Gifford and Whittredge, would also ride obligatorily westward. This tendency to equate innovation with novel location reflected the restlessness that a school with landscape as its vehicle required from its followers.

In 1905 Whittredge, eighty-five years old and aware of the shortness of the day, reflected on the anxiety he felt on seeing again, in 1859, the once-familiar Catskills: "It was impossible for me to shut out from my eyes the works of the great landscape painters which I had so recently seen in Europe, while I knew well enough that

if I was to succeed I must produce something new ... I was in despair."

The decade of the 1860s and the first half of the 1870s was a period marked by complexity and contradiction. Bierstadt and Church's immense spectacles reached a peak of popularity, while Kensett and Gifford continued their Luminist experimentations. At the same time, a landscape movement in dogmatic reaction against exper-

On the Cache La Poudre River, Colorado

WORTHINGTON WHITTREDGE. *1876; detail. The Amon Carter Museum, Fort Worth, Texas.* Whittredge's serene vision of the West contrasts with Bierstadt's bravura mountain peaks and dazzling sunlight. Whittredge preferred to emphasize the open space of the plains "with the mountains in the distance." The overall composition and spidery tree branches of this arcadia on the plains bear comparison to *The Old Hunting Grounds*.

The Rocky Mountains, Lander's Peak

ALBERT BIERSTADT. *1863; oil on canvas; 73 1/2 x 120 3/4 in. (187 x 307 cm). Metropolitan Museum of Art, Rogers Fund, 1907, (07.123).* Completed in New York, this large-scale and detailed panorama in the style Bierstadt favored was among the first highly dramatic landscapes to result from the painter's 1859 visit to the Wind River mountains in the Nebraska Territory. Bierstadt accurately records a Shoshone encampment below the majestically soaring mountains.

imentation had been active since 1863. These were the painters of the Society for the Advancement of Truth in Art, whose hard-line Ruskinian doctrine was advanced in the pages of its journal, the *New Path*.

Their conception of the new involved a radical opposition to art itself if art meant individual imaginative expression or the operation of subjectivity on nature beyond exact mirroring of the object perceived. With evangelical fervor, they contended that to think otherwise was simply immoral. They did what they could to take literally Emerson's Transcendental experience of nature: "All mean egotism vanishes. I become a transparent eyeball; I am nothing; I see all."

"New Path" painters Aaron Draper Shattuck (1832–1928), William Trost Richards (1833–1928), and Charles Herbert Moore (1840–1930) were to labor with missionary zeal at unmediated depictions of "every blade of grass that waves ... every beautiful pebble that rolls and rattles." Whittredge, strikingly candid in his memoirs, wrote, "Ruskin ... had told these tyros nothing could be too literal in the way of studies, and many of them believed Ruskin."

Meanwhile, influences from the faraway French village of Barbizon, which had been gathering momentum since 1850, began their infiltration, eventually altering public taste and ultimately ushering the Hudson River School into the past.

Seal Rock

ALBERT BIERSTADT. *c. 1872;*
41 1/2 x 56 1/2 in. (105 x 144 cm).
New Britain Museum of American Art,
Connecticut. Alix W. Stanley Fund.
An example of Bierstadt's later,
still-sensationalist, work, this is a
scene of America's Pacific Coast.
The translucent green wave about
to reach the frolicking seals on
their rock demonstrates his skill
at rendering natural phenomena
at sea as well as on the prairie.

Bierstadt: From Düsseldorf to Yosemite

Although he grew up in the whaling town of New Bedford, Massachusetts, Albert Bierstadt was born in Germany in 1830, and a large measure of his fame derived from studying in his family's home city of Düsseldorf. Düsseldorf style—Romantic and realist—represented the cutting edge of fashion in landscape painting by the time Bierstadt returned to America in 1857.

During this period Whittredge, then a member of the National Academy of Design, and William Stanley Haseltine (1835–1900) had been attracted to the German city known for its fine arts tradition. In 1856 Bierstadt, Whittredge, Haseltine, and Emanuel Leutze (1816–1868) took a working trip down the Rhine. In 1856–1857, Bierstadt and Whittredge wintered in Rome, where Gifford later joined them. At Gifford's suggestion, he and Bierstadt made a climb into the Apennines to study mountainous terrain.

Bierstadt's ability to sketch with speed and economy often produced drawings of enduring charm, but it also enabled him to take back to New Bedford a sizable portfolio of the European picturesque. In Massachusetts, he completed the paintings *Bay of Sorrento, Arch of Octavian, Street Scene in Rome*, and *Eternal City*. The most well-received picture culled from his European travels happened to be one of his first. This was *Sunshine and Shadow*, with its Romantic leitmotiv of a moss-covered church, an ancient tree, and the figure of an old woman—a chance discovery made during a walking tour through Hesse-Cassel, in Germany.

Sunrise, Yosemite Valley
ALBERT BIERSTADT *n.d.;*
oil on canvas; 36 1/2 x 52 1/2 in.
(93 x 133 cm). Amon Carter
Museum, Fort Worth, Texas.
Fitz Hugh Ludlow, who accompanied Bierstadt on his visit in 1863 to the Yosemite Valley, described painters in the chasm: "Sitting in their divine workshop ... a little after sunrise our artists began labor in that only method that can ever make a true painter or a living landscape." Bierstadt strikingly silhouettes trees against the dawn.

Emigrants Crossing the Plains

ALBERT BIERSTADT, *1867; oil on canvas;
60 x 96 in. (152 x 244 cm). The National
Cowboy Hall of Fame and Western Heritage
Center, Oklahoma City.* In 1863, while heading
for Fort Kearny, Nebraska, Bierstadt encountered
a wagon train of German immigrants bound
for Oregon. Bierstadt, unlike Cole or Church,
portrayed Indians and settlers plainly within
the context of the western scenery his paintings
glorified. The setting sun is directly in the
pioneers' path as they proceed through a gate-
way of trees on one side and cliffs on the other.

On April 12, 1861, secessionist South Carolina opened fire on the federal gar-
rison at Fort Sumter and the Civil War had begun. Although some critics claim
to have detected them, glyphs of the war's impact on the American spirit have yet
to be clearly uncovered in American landscape art during and immediately following the conflict. Unlike Gifford, who enlisted in the Seventh New York
Regiment, Bierstadt did not serve in the military. He visited the Army of the
Potomac in 1861 and, in the autumn of that year, with Leutze, toured battle sites
in the Washington area. One result, *The Bombardment of Fort Sumter* (1862), is a
strangely detached panorama rather than a scene of violence.

It was Lander's search for an alternative to the Oregon Trail—the Over-
land Trail to the North Platte and on to Fort Laramie in Wyoming—that gave
Bierstadt the requisite content for the vastness of scale he would always
favor. Back in New York, at the Tenth Street Building, he painted *The Rocky
Mountains, Lander's Peak* (1863), and *Thunderstorm in the Rocky Mountains*
(1866). Tuckerman raved, "No more genuine and grand American work has
been produced in landscape art." *The Rocky Mountains* would be exhibited in

1864 with Church's *The Heart of the Andes* at the New York Sanitary Fair as two monumental wonders of the world.

In 1863, with author Fitz Hugh Ludlow, Bierstadt visited Yosemite Valley and California. This trip yielded a series of Yosemite views: *The Domes of the Yosemite, Looking Down the Yosemite,* and *Valley of the Yosemite.* With his works fetching prices of up to $25,000 and $35,000, he entered a stratospheric earnings bracket among American artists. In Irvington, on the Hudson, the artist built an elaborate stone and marble mansion. The house burned in 1882, causing him to relocate to New York.

Bierstadt's reputation continued its ascent through the mid-1870s but by 1889, *The Last of the Buffalo* was refused by the selection committee of the Paris Exposition. His art had met with its own kind of extinction. Bierstadt died in New York in 1902.

Sunset in the Yosemite Valley

ALBERT BIERSTADT. *1868; oil on canvas; 35 1/2 x 51 1/2 in. (90 x 131 cm). The Haggin Museum, Stockton, California.* Bierstadt excelled at depictions of mountainous grandeur. Here, his customary Romantic sense of the sublime captures the climax of day's end in the Yosemite Valley. Beneath a mass of low clouds, the still-blazing sun fills the valley with an orange glow. With the cliffs resembling European castles, the spires of redwoods accentuate the upward trajectory of the chasm.

Whittredge, Gifford, Kensett, and the West

Thomas Worthington Whittredge, born in Springfield, Ohio, in 1820, toiled as a portrait painter in Cincinnati and Indianapolis while cultivating his own landscape style in the early 1840s. Sanford Robinson Gifford, born in 1823 in Greenfield, New York, was, by the mid-1840s, studying formally in New York with John Rubens Smith and sketching scenery in the Catskills and Berkshires.

In essence, Gifford's development as a painter followed a pattern seemingly ordained by Cole and Durand. By 1847 the American Art Union and the National Academy of Design already had exhibited his work, and a year prior to going abroad in 1855, Gifford was named a member of the National Academy. Although Whittredge was in Europe for a decade, studying in the urban galleries of The Hague, Antwerp, and Berlin, as well as confronting nature directly in the Italian, German, and Swiss countryside, he considered Gifford a first-rate adventurer.

Gifford made it as far as the Nile, Constantinople, and Athens during a second excursion from 1868 to 1869. Having chosen England as his first stop—to meet John Ruskin and admire Turner's work—he returned to New York from his initial European experience in 1857, taking quarters in the Tenth Street Building. No sign of impulsiveness, however, disturbs the muted radiance and understated foreground of the unmistakably Luminist

Kaaterskill Clove, in the Catskills (1862), whose qualities find earliest expression in *Lake Nemi,* completed in Rome in 1856.

Whittredge, also working in the Tenth Street Building, threw himself into reclaiming his sense of American scenery, a feat he carried off in *The Old Hunting Grounds* (1864), with its decaying canoe sheltered by trees sparkling with sunlight. In 1866, three years before the completion of the Transcontinental Railroad, Whittredge decided to make the journey west—to Colorado and New Mexico. Four years earlier, with the passage of the Homestead Act, settlers had begun streaming into the prairie. Whittredge joined General John Pope's Military Division of the Missouri, riding on horseback for two thousand miles.

From Fort Leavenworth, Kansas, the soldiers and the artist rode the Oregon Trail, taking the North Platte route to Denver, where Whittredge made sketches of the river. These formed the basis for *Crossing the Ford, the North Platte, Colorado* (1870) and *Crossing the River Platte.* His drawings of the Cache La Poudre river culminated in *On the Cache La Poudre* (1868) and *Cache La Poudre River, Colorado* (1876). What Whittredge described as "the appearance everywhere of an innocent, primitive existence" made the plains, not the mountains, his favorite western theme. His canvas *Santa Fe* (1866), with Indians prominent in the foreground, is elongated to encompass the plains and is vibrant with a painterly earthen impasto.

Accompanied by Gifford and Kensett, Whittredge went again to Colorado and Wyoming in July 1870—this time by train. Never having ventured beyond the

On the Cache La Poudre River, Colorado
WORTHINGTON WHITTREDGE. *1876; oil on canvas; 40 3/8 x 60 3/8 in. (103 x 153 cm).*
Amon Carter Museum, Fort Worth, Texas.
Painted after Whittredge's second trip to Colorado with Kensett and Gifford in 1870, this landscape was based on an earlier study from his journey in 1866 with General John Pope's Colorado expedition. Never a full-fledged Luminist, Whittredge allows his brushwork to luxuriate in the lush greens and browns of this river scene.

The Old Hunting Grounds
WORTHINGTON WHITTREDGE. *1864; oil on canvas; 36 x 27 in. (91 x 69 cm).*
Reynolda House Museum of American Art, Winston-Salem, North Carolina.
Having returned from Europe in 1859, Whittredge set to work acclimatizing himself to American scenery. Before his search for the new took him to Colorado and New Mexico, Whittredge showed a unique sense of composition in this view inside a glittering forest cathedral that reveals an abandoned canoe on a still pool.

Valley of the Chug Water, Wyoming Territory, Aug. 9th 1870
SANFORD R. GIFFORD. *1870; oil and canvas; 7 3/4 x 12 7/8 in (20 x 33 cm). Courtesy of Amon Carter Museum, Fort Worth, Texas.* Gifford quickly joined Dr. Ferdinand V. Hayden's survey expedition in the Wyoming Territory after arriving in Colorado with Whittredge and Kensett. Though his output was small, while in the West, Gifford found the vast geometric forms and flat plains suited to his Luminist style.

Missouri, Kensett remained stonily unmoved by the West. For Gifford, however, the West was an entirely new experience. In the heat of summer, he decided to strike out on his own with Dr. Ferdinand V. Hayden's geological survey expedition to Utah and the Wyoming Territory. Although photographer William Henry Jackson, artist Henry Wood Elliott, and Gifford traveled along the Lodgepole, Sweetwater, Chug Water, Platte, and Green rivers, Gifford's output was not prolific. Only eight of his western landscapes have been recovered. Unlike Whittredge, who enthusiastically adjusted his style to the West, Gifford held to Luminist standards in his *Valley of the Chug Water, Wyoming Territory, Aug. 9th 1870,* placing its looming subject within modest dimensions.

Thomas Moran and Yellowstone

In 1871 another painter joined Hayden's caravan in the Wyoming Territory's Yellowstone region. Thomas Moran's contribution to the western landscape and the westward migration of Hudson River School aesthetics is perhaps rivaled only by Bierstadt himself. Born in 1837 in Lancashire, England, the place of Cole's birth, Moran arrived in America in 1844.

Having devoted considerable study to Turner, Moran claimed to be a Ruskinian in as much as he followed Ruskin's protocol of relating a "true impression" of nature in his landscapes. But for Moran there was a sharp distinction to be made between rendering a scene literally and conveying its "true impression." He asserted that "literal transcripts from Nature," as he called them, were utterly without value. Moran forthrightly declared his principles to be idealistic, not realistic, thus establishing an important link with Cole.

Moran, in fact, replaced Gifford, who turned down Hayden's request to go with his team to Yellowstone. According to Gifford's friend Jackson, who continued

Following page:
Our Old Mill
GEORGE INNESS. *1849; oil on canvas; 29 7/8 x 42 1/8 in. (76 x 107 cm). The Art Institute of Chicago, Goodman Fund, (1939.388).* A month's study with Régis Gignoux in 1846 probably had little effect on the self-taught Inness's early naturalism, so much in evidence in this shadow-drenched view of trees beside a mill stream. This landscape shows primarily the influence of Cole and Durand, but by 1850 he would become aware of Barbizon painter Théodore Rousseau.

Western Landscape
THOMAS MORAN. *1864; oil on canvas; 29 x 44 in. (74 x 112 cm). The New Britain Museum of American Art, Connecticut. Charles F. Smith Fund.* English immigrant Thomas Moran, whose greatest influences were J. M. W. Turner and American marine painter James Hamilton, visited the Great Lakes region in 1860— ten years before touring the Far West. Formerly called *The Wilds of Lake Superior,* this picture's heroic cataract and turbulent sky show something of Cole as well as Turner.

Cliffs of the Green River
THOMAS MORAN. *1874; detail. The Amon Carter Museum , Fort Worth, Texas.* Moran depicts Hayden's expeditioners as they view the weather-carved sandstone cliffs. Initially daunted by the colors he observed in the Yellowstone region and Grand Canyon, he successfully applied his study of J. M. W. Turner to the arid topography of the American West. Moran reexamined this location in several subsequent paintings, such as *Cliffs of the Upper Colorado, Wyoming Territory* (1882).

his photographic duties for Hayden, the seemingly frail painter amazed his wilderness-toughened colleagues with his endurance and resourcefulness. Reaching Fort Ellis, on the periphery of what is now Yellowstone National Park, Moran remarked that he expected no "finer general view of the Rocky Mountains."

Before reaching the Grand Canyon, which Moran at first thought was untranslatable into art, the expeditioners had seen the Devil's Slide, Mammoth Hot Springs, and Tower Falls. As the survey team departed from Yellowstone, Moran made dynamic watercolor sketches as the expeditioners inspected Old Faithful, the Castle Geyser, and the cliffs of the Green River.

The press, from Denver's *Rocky Mountain News* to the *Times* of London, responded with encouraging reviews with each new chromolithograph made from Moran's investigations

In 1872 Moran went to Yosemite, which he found, anticlimactically, to be the provenance of Bierstadt. The following year, however, the artist, to his fortune, joined Colonel John Wesley Powell's journey down the Colorado River. The immense *Grand Canyon of the Yellowstone* (1872) and *The Chasm of the Colorado* (1873–1874) are the two great testaments to Moran's zeal for the West. Named to the National Academy of Design in 1884, the artist died in 1926.

Cliffs of the Green River

THOMAS MORAN. *1874; oil on canvas; 25 1/8 x 45 3/8 in. (64 x 115 cm). The Amon Carter Museum, Fort Worth, Texas.* Moran was astonished by the sight of these cliffs in south-western Wyoming while on his way to join Dr. Ferdinand V. Hayden's U.S. Geological Survey expedition into Yellowstone in 1871. Known for its desolateness as the Green River Badlands, this region's sandstone formations appealed to Moran's sense of the sublime.

September Afternoon
GEORGE INNESS. *1887; oil on canvas; 37 1/2 x 29 in. (95 x 74 cm). National Museum of Art, Smithsonian Institution, Gift of William T. Evans. Art Resource, New York.* Inness's style as a painter oscillated between earlier classical modes and increasing experimentation with color and form. This landscape epitomizes Inness in an experimental mood. Soft, billowing forms are used for both clouds and trees. The greens and blues are intense, the flowers reminiscent of Barbizon painter Corot.

The Last of the Hudson River School Painters

In 1839 the school of painting galvanized by Thomas Cole was advancing apace in America, but in France, at the French Academy of Sciences, artists saw for the first time the remarkable invention of Louis Jacques Daguerre. One horrified witness, the teacher of Régis Gignoux, pronounced painting to be dead and the daguerreotype its executioner.

After settling in America, Gignoux (1816–1882), a realist, adapted quickly to the Hudson River School's then-prevailing attention to minutiae. In Brooklyn, New York, in 1846, he was to provide George Inness with the only formal instruction the painter would receive. The following year, Inness went to Europe.

Inness is noteworthy for his durability and originality during a period of transition—not only for America's landscape art but for the nation's painters in general. The radical dualism found in the Swedenborgian mysticism of which he was a passionate adherent seems to complement the notion of two Innesses: the first, who began as a follower of Cole and Durand's naturalism, the second, a painter who dissolved the hard outlines of forms into surrounding space.

Although Inness's *The Shadow of the Valley of Death* was an homage to Cole's moral expositions, his following of Cole and Durand was never blind despite having derived his initial understanding of painting entirely from the Hudson River School. In the two years prior to visiting Italy for the first time, Inness had exhibited views of the Newark, New Jersey, area and the Schuylkill River at the Art Union and National Academy. At twenty, he was seen as an emerging talent. Subsequent exposure to the magisterial classicism of Claude and Poussin made only

On the Delaware River
GEORGE INNESS. *1861–1863; oil on canvas; 28 3/4 x 48 1/4 in. (73 x 123 cm). The Brooklyn Museum.* Dwelling for a time on views of the Delaware River, Inness began to fuse classical Italian composition with an emerging new approach to basic landscape elements. The piebald clouds, for example, are unlike those of his American contemporaries. This landscape does not suppress the reality of an expanding human presence, as evidenced by the steaming locomotive.

Cupid and Psyche
WILLIAM PAGE. *1843; oil on canvas; 10 7/8 x 14 3/4 in. (28 x 38 cm). M. H. de Young Memorial Museum, San Francisco, California.* A fiercely independent thinker who introduced Hudson River School painter George Inness to the spiritual system of Swedenborg, Page painted these two figures from a marble sculpture he saw in Rome. The angle chosen to show the couple's erotic embrace, along with the mysterious forest in the background, creates a powerful and voyeuristic dreamscape.

slight inroads into a style still bent on the rather crabbed, exacting brushwork that prevailed among Cole and Durand's disciples. The early *Landscape* (1848) and *The Old Mill* (1849), however, show a certain classical imprint.

In 1850 Inness happened to be in Paris to witness the excitement surrounding "a little picture," as he called it, by Théodore Rousseau, soon to become an eminent figure among the Barbizon painters. At the time, Inness saw little cause for all the commotion.

Long before his work began to be associated with that of Rousseau and Narcise Virgile Diaz de La Peña, Inness claimed to have disconnected meaning from detail prior to ever going to Europe.

By 1861, with the completion of *On the Delaware River*, Inness had achieved a confidence and independence that allowed him to oscillate spontaneously between his earlier methods and an ethereal new world of painting. In 1863, having left Brooklyn and moved to Medfield, Massachusetts, he threw down the gauntlet with nature-first detractors at the *New Path*. Before a show in Boston, he published a piece in which he incorporated favorable notices from Jarves, the *New Path's* most outspoken antagonist.

Behind the canvases Jarves regarded as authentically American in spirit stood a sensibility easily overlooked in the history of native landscape. "A work of art does not appeal to the intellect. It does not appeal to the moral sense. Its aim is not to instruct, not to edify but to waken an emotion," Inness wrote. Rather than a repudiation of Hudson River School tradition, Inness's statement can be taken as a reaffirmation of the sublime in a new epoch.

It was probably in 1866 that Inness was introduced to the spiritualism of Emanuel Swedenborg by William Page (1811–1885), a portrait painter sometimes called "the American Titian" who became well-known among the many so-called eccentrics of nineteenth-century American art. Page, who extrapolated a system of proportion from the Bible, devised a color theory through which he attempted to animate his images with a life of their own. From the 1870s onward, Inness's Swedenborgian faith intensified. It remains a matter purely of speculation whether the Swedish mystic's writings on space in the spirit world correlates to Inness's experiments with simplification of color and softening of forms.

During the 1870s, in works such as *The Rigour of the Game* (1875), *The Coming Storm* and *Durham, Connecticut*, both from 1878, Inness revisited earlier classicism while infusing it with qualities that evoke comparisons to Camille Corot and the Barbizon painters—comparisons the artist adamantly resisted. He also denounced Impressionism, another movement with which critics associated him.

From the late 1880s, with *Harvest Moon*, to the almost monochromatic *Home of the Heron*, completed three years before his death in 1894, Inness created landscapes both intimate and remote, more internal than external in vision, and bordering on the abstract while generating illumination seemingly from within. In 1895 the *New York Evening Post* offered the conclusion that "not even Rousseau . . . could make him pay the compliment of imitation, or assimilation. He followed no one."

The movement that had motivated so many painters and built a constituency for American art by selectively synthesizing European tradition with American natural grandeur was now in twilight. As early as 1877, Whittredge, openly proud of having been one of the stalwarts of the Hudson River School, worried about his prospects. He rightly suspected that irrelevance was stalking him and his breed.

The spotlight increasingly shone on the Europeans Diaz, Rousseau, Corot, and Charles Daubigny (1817–1878), a painter whom Whittredge admired. The turn of the century closed on the memory of Bierstadt and Church and placed Cole and Durand into a reliquary of obscurity. The Romanticism that had kindled the American imagination and induced artists to seek out images of American identity and lofty moral purpose on the frontier's horizon was at an end. Modernism was to have its day, and, with it, American painters would eventually emerge to dominate the Abstract Expressionist movement of the 1940s and 1950s.

During the nineteenth century, the label Hudson River School was apparently intended as a brickbat hurled at the followers of Thomas Cole by a hostile journalist. Yet it was during the mid-twentieth-century heyday of America's avant-garde "action painters" that interest in the lost masters of American landscape suddenly revived. Their rediscovery is ongoing, and they continue to be known as the Hudson River School.

Niagara
GEORGE INNESS. *1889; oil on canvas; 30 x 45 in. (76 x 114 cm). National Museum of American Art, Washington, D. C.* Together with a comparable view of Niagara Falls painted on wood four years earlier, this landscape suggests that Inness saw the majestic falls as a source for his most daring and visionary work. Inness's heavy brush renders the falls as a plummeting mass of green, blue, and white. He also shows a chimney oozing smoke into a gray sky.

September Afternoon
GEORGE INNESS. *detail; 1887. National Museum of Art, Washington, D. C.*
An example of Inness's extravagant departure from Hudson River School norms, this landscape does not rely on a grand spectacle of untouched wilderness. With a palette free from realistic constraints, Inness situates globular trees amid an intimate scene composed of brilliant colors. The figures on the grass are almost ghostlike, appearing not to be of this world

INDEX

INDEX (continued)

FURTHER READING

The Friends of Historic Kingston. *Jervis McEntee: Kingston's Artist of the Hudson River School.* Black Dome Press, Corporation © 2015.

Kevin J. Avery, Oswaldo Rodriguez Roque, John K. Howat, Doreen Bolger Burke, and Catherine Hoover Voorsanger. *American Paradise: The World of the Hudson River School.* Yale University Press © 2013.

Kevin J. Avery, Franklin Kelly, and Claire A. Conway. *Hudson River School Visions: The Landscapes of Sanford R. Gifford.* Yale University Press © 2013.

Judith Hansen O'Toole and Arnold Skolnick. *Different Views in Hudson River School Painting.* Columbia University Press © 2008.

Barbara Babcock Millhouse. *American Wilderness: The Story of the Hudson River School of Painting.* Black Dome Press, Corporation © 2007.

INTERNET RESOURCES

The Met—The Hudson River School

https://www.metmuseum.org/toah/hd/hurs/hd_hurs.htm

The Hudson River School

http://hrs-art.com/

Encyclopedia Britannica—Hudson River School

https://www.britannica.com/art/Hudson-River-school

Hudson River School Art Trail

http://www.hudsonriverschool.org/

U.S. History—Hudson River School Artists

http://www.ushistory.org/us/26e.asp

EDUCATIONAL VIDEOS

Access these videos with your smartphone or use the URLs below to find them online.

 PBS introduces the Hudson River School, comprising a group of American painters led by British born artist Thomas Cole who forged an artistic vision of the American wilderness.

 Take a tour of the New York Historical Society to uncover a better understanding of the Hudson River School and the artistic processes of icons including Thomas Cole and Asher B. Durand.

 CNN introduces you to the Hudson River School artists and the landscapes that inspired them.

 Art historian Linda S. Ferber describes the importance of landscape, and the fate of the wilderness, to Hudson River School painter Thomas Cole.

 Listen in on a conversations with experts from the New York Historical Society about nature and American vision through the eyes of the Hudson School artists.